Scholastic BookFiles

A READING GUIDE TO

Tuck Everlasting

by Natalie Babbitt

Hannah Mitchell

SCHOLASTIC REFERENCE

Library of Congress Cataloging-in-Publication Data

Scholastic BookFiles: A reading guide to Tuck Everlasting by Natalie Babbitt/Hannah Mitchell.   p. cm.

Summary: Discusses the writing, characters, plot, and themes of this 1975 novel. Includes discussion questions and activities. Includes bibliographical references (p.).

1. Babbitt, Natalie. Tuck Everlasting—Juvenile literature.
2. Immortalism in literature—Juvenile literature.
[1. Babbitt, Natalie. Tuck Everlasting.   2. American literature— History and criticism.]   I. Title.   II. Series.

PS3552.A1735T85   2004

813′.54—dc21   2003050391

0-439-53821-1

10 9 8 7 6 5 4 3 2 1   04 05 06 07 08

Composition by Brad Walrod/High Text Graphics, Inc.
Cover and interior design by Red Herring Design

Printed in the U.S.A.   23
First printing, March 2004

Contents

About Natalie Babbitt

"There's always one best word, if you
listen for it."

—Natalie Babbitt

Natalie Babbitt is an artist in more ways than one. Known
by many people for her descriptive, metaphorical writing,
she is less well known for her beautiful illustrations. However,
it was this passion that involved her in children's books in the
first place.

Born in Dayton, Ohio, on July 28, 1932, Natalie Zane Moore
[Babbitt] came into the world at the height of the Great
Depression. Thanks to her parents, though, she and her sister
enjoyed a life filled with good times, books, and loads of loving
encouragement. Natalie loved drawing from an early age. Though
she read books constantly, she had very little interest in writing
them. She wanted only to illustrate, to bring words to life. She
dreamed of capturing imaginations the very same way her
imagination had been taken captive by the illustrations in *Alice's
Adventures in Wonderland*, one of her favorite books. With her
mother's support, Natalie was able to develop her passion and
her talent. She also had a great deal of support from her teachers

at Laurel School in Cleveland. After high school, she went on to study art at Smith College in Northampton, Massachusetts.

Love interrupted her art career and Natalie married Samuel Fisher Babbitt, an academic administrator, right after her college graduation. They spent the next ten years in Connecticut, Tennessee, and Washington, D.C., where Babbitt raised their children, Christopher, Tom, and Lucy.

Eventually, Babbitt got back to drawing when she illustrated a book written by her husband, called *The Forty-Ninth Magician*. They thought it was the beginning of an ideal collaboration. However, after moving to Clinton, New York, her husband's career responsibilities left him with little time to dedicate to his writing. So Natalie Babbitt decided that if she wanted to create books for children, she would simply have to write *and* illustrate them herself. Her first two picture books, *Dick Foote and the Shark* and *Phoebe's Revolt*, were written in easy rhyme, a style Natalie thought suited her better than prose.

Babbitt's faith in herself as an artist and a writer turned out to be momentous for her and for readers everywhere. Though she started by writing and illustrating picture books for younger children, soon one of her ideas developed into the novel that would eventually make her one of the preeminent children's novelists of our time. In that novel, *The Search for Delicious*, Babbitt incorporated her love of fairy tales. The book was greeted by children's book reviewers as the first major work of an exciting new talent.

Natalie Babbitt's subsequent books have consistently achieved a place on the major lists of outstanding children's literature in the years of their publication. *The Devil's Storybook* was nominated for a National Book Award in 1975, named an American Library Association (ALA) Notable Book, and received the Christopher and Lewis Carroll Shelf awards. *Kneeknock Rise* was a Newbery Honor Book in 1971; *Goody Hall* was chosen as an Honor Book in the 1971 Book World Children's Spring Book Festival; and two of Babbitt's books have been selected for inclusion in the Children's Book Council's Children's Book Showcase: *Goody Hall* in 1972 and *More Small Poems*, illustrated by Babbitt and written by poet Valerie Worth, in 1977. In 1981, Babbitt was the U.S. nominee for the Hans Christian Andersen Medal, an award presented by the International Board on Books for Young People in recognition of someone "whose complete works have made a lasting contribution to children's literature." (This award is "the highest international recognition given to an author and an illustrator of children's books.") All of these books, including *The Eyes of the Amaryllis,* were also ALA Notable Children's Books.

Natalie Babbitt is perhaps best known for her magical book, *Tuck Everlasting.* Babbitt has brought books to life for children just as she had always hoped she would. She has created worlds that mesh fantasy and reality. She allows readers to go to places that might not be real exactly, but are certainly true to life.

"Winnie blinked, and all at once her mind was drowned with understanding of what he was saying. For she—yes, even she—would go out of the world willy-nilly someday. Just go out, like the flame of a candle, and no use protesting. It was a certainty."

—Tuck Everlasting

There comes a moment in all young people's lives when they realize that they are not going to live forever. Whether the thought is prompted by the death of a beloved pet or of a relative or friend, the realization changes the person. This is why Natalie Babbitt felt compelled to write about death—or in this case, life without death and its implications.

Babbitt says, "I think it's something that everyone thinks of from the time when they realize they can't [live forever]. Even before you're six because you have a pet or a grandmother [whom you've lost] and you begin to wonder about it. So I thought it would be interesting to write a book about real people, ordinary people—not like the people in fairy tales who are always living happily ever after. But, what would [living forever] really be like in the real world."

In *Tuck Everlasting*, Babbitt created Winnie, a character who feels that her life is meaningless and boring. The prospect of living forever is exciting to her. In the course of the novel, as she gets to know the Tucks, Winnie listens to different opinions about eternal life: Jesse is hopeful, Miles is realistic, Mae is determined, and Angus is depressed. Winnie comes to understand that eternal life might be a curse and not a blessing.

This novel is Babbitt's way of introducing the life cycle and explaining the beauty of living in the moment. Babbitt seems to say that life is short and your time on earth ought to be meaningful in some way.

Babbitt says, "[*Tuck Everlasting*] presents dilemmas, and I think that's what life does! I dealt with a lot of dilemmas before I even started school. I think a lot of adults would like to think that things are simple for kids, but that's not so. . . . I think the book doesn't present any lessons about what's right and what's wrong, but it does point out how difficult these decisions are."

About *Tuck Everlasting*

◆ *You have said that you are always surprised when people find this story unusual. You think eternal life is quite an ordinary dilemma to think about. Why then do you think the issue is so compelling to both children and adults?*

It's very interesting when I go to schools and talk to students. They are so direct and they usually say, well yes it would be neat [to live forever] but I wouldn't want to do that because x, y, and z. All the same reasons I would give. And once in a while I get a child who is very upset by the ending and we talk about that, too. There is no right or wrong way to look at it. I tell them that at different times in your life you feel differently about it.

◆ *You have noted that some readers have not been satisfied with the ending. Why do you think some readers aren't satisfied with Winnie's choice?*

It is mainly girls who feel that way. They have been quite charmed by Jesse and they think she should marry him. I always have a good laugh about that because he is charming but I think he'd make a terrible husband!

But most of them do change their minds about it later on. In fact, a young girl wrote to tell me that she was so very disappointed with the ending and I wrote back to her to say that that was okay—there is no right or wrong way to feel. Seven years later, the same girl wrote to me and said that she had changed her mind, and that she realized the book had ended the way it was supposed to. I always tell kids about that because that's beautiful.

◆ *You have said that* Tuck Everlasting *doesn't exactly teach a lesson; rather, that it presents dilemmas. Does that mean that you think there is no right or wrong answer to the biggest dilemma of the book? Doesn't* Tuck Everlasting *disapprove of someone choosing eternal life over natural death?*

Winnie does what I would have done. There are plenty of people who wouldn't have done it, though. Particularly if there was someone to share eternity with. I think it would be very boring, and even with the right person I think it would be lonely. The fact that we don't have a lot of time puts a lot of delicious pressure on us to do things. But there's no law that says that's the way you have to feel about it.

◆ *The book has an anyplace, anytime feel to it. Do you think the setting is important to the story?*

Although I am from Ohio, *Tuck Everlasting* is based mainly on upstate New York. I can remember learning that there was a forest that went on through about five different states. I always thought that was pretty interesting and that's what Winnie's grandmother says. So I had that in mind, also. But Tuck's house and pond are based on a real place that we owned years ago. It doesn't really matter, though. The book could be set anywhere that isn't desert or mountain. The wood is the important part.

◆ *Some people have said that you essentially "turn religion on its head" in this novel. Did religion come into play for you? Are you surprised that some people read it that way?*

I thought [that interpretation] was extremely interesting because I had never thought about that. Formal religion has always been a difficulty for me in terms of figuring it out. I like things to be spelled out. I read a lot of Greek and Roman myths as a child— that was my favorite kind of reading in addition to fairy tales— and I always felt that the logic in those stories was much more obvious than the logic in the Bible because you didn't have to be perfect. I had a lot of trouble with that as a child. I couldn't be perfect. So, I don't know how much of a role that played in the book. But it might well be in there. I don't object to that.

Tuck Everlasting is a different type of fantasy than [the type] kids these days are accustomed to. In fact, it is the simple fact that living forever is an option that places this book in the fantasy genre.

◆ *Does the imagery you use in your writing come from being an artist? For example, in* Tuck Everlasting *you describe August as*

*having "blank white dawns and glaring noons, and sunsets
smeared with too much color."*

I guess there is a picturesque quality that comes into play and
that probably does come from the same place. My mother was a
painter and she trained my sister and me to look at things early
on. It probably comes from that, too. I am a relatively passive
person, so I love to look at things. That part is fun.

◆ *You have said that you use metaphors and similes because they
help readers understand things that they otherwise might not. But
what about personification? It seems to come into play a lot in this
book. For example, grass is "forlorn," the house is "proud of itself,"
and the cows are "wise." Where does that come from for you?*

We were a word-loving family. It probably comes from my father
more than anywhere else. He did very funny things with language
in that way.

About being a writer

◆ *Will you describe your writing process?*

I have to get everything all figured out in my head before I start.
How [the story] will begin and end, who the characters are, what
their names are, where it will happen—all the details of that
kind. I write straight through then, although it takes me quite a
long time because I rewrite as I go along. There aren't any rules
about how to do it.

◆ *You have been criticized for being too descriptive. How do you feel about that?*

Well, perhaps some of the books are wordier than they need to be. That's hard for some people.

◆ *Do you write every day?*

No. I used to. Although, I never was a fast writer. It takes me a year to write a novel and that's not counting the time it takes me to plan it out.

◆ *What happens when you get blocked?*

I've never been in much of a hurry. The writer's block comes for me when I can't work out a plot. The rest of it, the writing, I really enjoy and I find that relatively easy. We all use words all the time, so it's a universal thing for us. But I get hung up on plots—plotting is hard for me.

◆ *What are you working on now?*

I've got about two more ideas and that will be it.

◆ *How did you become a writer?*

I originally wanted to be an illustrator, so my husband wrote the first book. But he didn't want to do that anymore because he was busy. He is more of a people person and he just couldn't be alone as much as you have to. No one ever said to me in a writing class that being alone is a part of it [being a writer], but it certainly is. You have to like to be by yourself.

So, I figured I could write books in verse because I had always written a lot of verse—not poetry but verse [verse is a form of writing in which words are arranged in a rhythmic pattern but is less structured than traditional poetry]. So, the first two books I did were in verse. I had a lot of fun with those but then my editor said that I would have a lot more freedom if I were writing in prose, so I sat down to write a little picture-book story and it just kept getting bigger and bigger and bigger and became *The Search for Delicious.*

It might sound silly but I [wrote a novel] before I knew how hard it was to do. After that, it became more difficult and it continues to become more difficult because you're more conscious of what you're doing and that makes it hard. Writing is extremely hard work.

◆ *Does the acclaim that you've received put pressure on you when you sit down to write a new book?*

Ambition is a strange thing. I never had very much. I just wanted to do one book. But there are a lot of things I like to do. I like to make things, knit, and play the piano. So, I wasn't particularly single-minded about it.

◆ *What happened to the idea of being an artist?*

I wanted to be an artist, but it seemed clear to me early on that I was adequate, but that was all I was ever going to be. We have a lot of marvelous illustrators, [Maurice] Sendak being my favorite. I actually think we have more fine illustrators than we have fine writers.

◆ *Did you always know that you wanted to do books for children?*

Oh yes, and that's because of *Alice in Wonderland.* John Tenniel's illustrations in the original *Alice in Wonderland* just knocked my socks off! Those pictures are very beautiful and very funny and that's such a wonderful combination. You see that a lot now, but when I was a child, they were either cartoons or incredible paintings.

◆ *When did you start to think about what you would be when you grew up?*

I wanted to be a librarian when I was in second grade, and then in fourth grade I decided I wanted to be an illustrator. I have a huge respect for librarians and teachers. It is some of the most important work anybody can do. My daughter is a teacher for second grade and she published three novels for teenagers—she's a great writer. I don't think I could have [taught] because I don't think I'm a "people" kind of person. I prefer to work alone. But thank God there are people who prefer to do that kind of work. We owe them so much.

Chapter Charter:
Questions to Guide Your Reading

The following questions will help you think about the important parts of each chapter.

Prologue
- How does the author describe the setting in this section?
- Why do you think she chooses to be so mysterious in the prologue?

Chapter 1
- How does the author's use of language help you to understand the setting?
- Why aren't the Fosters curious about the wood? If you were Winnie, do you think you might have wanted to explore the wood? Why or why not?

Chapter 2
- Why does Angus Tuck consider his dream about heaven a "good dream"?
- Why do you think Mae Tuck doesn't care about her appearance anymore?

Chapter 3
- What do you think Winnie's life is like? How does it compare to your life?

- Why does Winnie throw stones at the toad? What emotion do you think she is feeling?
- Why does Winnie tell the toad she wants to run away?

Chapter 4
- What is your first impression of the man in the yellow suit? Does the author give you any clues about his character?
- Where do you think the music that Winnie's grandmother hears comes from?

Chapter 5
- What do you think Jesse is thinking when he tries to prevent Winnie from drinking the spring water?
- What does Mae mean when she says, "The worst is happening at last"?

Chapter 6
- Why do the Tucks kidnap Winnie? What do you think you would have done in Winnie's place?
- Why does Winnie feel reassured when she hears the music box?

Chapter 7
- How had the Tucks figured out they were going to live forever?
- Why do you think the man in the yellow suit is following Winnie and the Tucks?

Chapter 8
- Why does Winnie begin to feel happy about being with the Tucks?

- The man in the yellow suit overhears the Tucks' story. What do you think he might be planning?

Chapter 9

- It takes many hours for Winnie, Mae, Jesse, and Miles to reach the Tucks' home. Why do you think they live in such a hard-to-reach place?
- Why do you think Angus Tuck is so happy to meet Winnie?

Chapter 10

- Do you think Mae thinks of her life as blessed or cursed? Why?
- Why is Winnie so amazed at the inside of the Tucks' home?

Chapter 11

- Why does Winnie suddenly want to go home?

Chapter 12

- Why does Angus Tuck take Winnie to the pond to talk to her?
- How is the movement of the pond water meaningful to their conversation about the life cycle?

Chapter 13

- Why do you think the man in the yellow suit goes to the Fosters instead of to the police?

Chapter 14

- Why does Winnie go back and forth, first liking the disorder of the Tucks' lifestyle, then longing for her regular bedtime routine?
- How do the Tucks make Winnie feel better?

- As Winnie tries to fall asleep, she can't decide whether or not to believe the Tucks' story. Would you have believed it? Why or why not?

Chapter 15
- Why do you think the man in the yellow suit wants to trade his knowledge of Winnie's whereabouts for the Fosters' wood?
- What do the man in the yellow suit's actions tell you about his character?

Chapter 16
- Why is the constable surprised that the Fosters agree to sell the wood?
- Is the constable suspicious of the man in the yellow suit's motives?

Chapter 17
- How does swatting a mosquito make Winnie realize that dying is a natural part of the life cycle?
- Why does Winnie insist that Miles throw the fish back?

Chapter 18
- Why do you think Miles conceals the reason that he and Winnie return without any fish?
- How have Winnie's feelings for the Tucks changed? Do you think she has stronger feelings for some of the Tucks than others?

Chapter 19

- Why does the man in the yellow suit see the Tucks as selfish?
- Mae Tuck hits the man over the head with the gun. Do you think she does the right thing? Does she have another option?

Chapter 20

- Why does Winnie lie to the constable?
- Angus Tuck stares at the man in the yellow suit after Mae hits him. What do you think he is thinking about? Why does Winnie seem horrified at Angus Tuck's reaction?

Chapter 21

- Do you think the Fosters regret selling the wood?
- What makes Winnie's family think she has changed?

Chapter 22

- Why does Winnie volunteer to help rescue Mae?
- Do you think Jesse should have given Winnie the spring water? Why or why not?

Chapter 23

- Why does being disheveled make Winnie's mother and grandmother more interesting?
- Why does Winnie feel so good and right about what she is about to do?

Chapter 24

- How do you think Winnie feels helping Mae escape?
- Do you think Winnie does the right thing in freeing Mae? Why?

Chapter 25

- How does Winnie's reputation in the village change after she helps Mae?
- Why do you think Winnie saves the toad from the dog?
- What important decision does Winnie make when she pours the spring water on the toad?

Epilogue

- How does the author connect Winnie and the Tucks at the end of the story?
- Why does Angus Tuck say, "Good girl," when he sees Winnie's grave?

Plot: What's Happening?

"Life's got to be lived, no matter how long or short...."

—Mae Tuck, *Tuck Everlasting*

Tuck Everlasting is the story of a young girl named Winnie whose life in the small town of Treegap turns magical when she explores the wood in search of adventure and independence. At the beginning of this novella, or short novel, Winnie Foster is bored. She wants something interesting to happen to her. Winnie looks to a toad in her front yard for advice. Should she run away? She resolves to think it over and decide in the morning.

That same evening, a man in a yellow suit comes by and engages Winnie in a conversation. He wants to know how long Winnie's family has lived in the area and if they know all their neighbors. Winnie has a bad feeling about him, which we learn when the narrator says that Winnie was "suddenly reminded of the stiff black ribbons they had hung on the door of the cottage for her grandfather's funeral." When she tells the man that her family has lived there "forever," he echoes the word *forever*. He tells her that he is looking for someone, a family to be specific. At that, Winnie's grandmother comes out and makes it clear that neither she nor her granddaughter talks with strangers. She is interrupted, though, by the faint sound of music, which she first heard many years ago and which she describes as "elf music."

The next morning, Winnie is still unwilling to make a final decision about running away. She decides to go for a short walk into the wood that her family owns but that she has never before bothered to explore. She will decide once she gets there if she's ever coming back. Soon, she comes upon Jesse Tuck taking a drink of water from a natural spring. He notices her and calls her out of her hiding place. When Winnie tries to drink from the same spring, he tries to stop her. To Jesse's relief, Mae and Miles Tuck arrive on horseback. Thinking quickly, the family kidnaps Winnie to prevent her from drinking the water from the spring. Winnie is scared and confused. Why is this nice family taking her away? Why wouldn't they let her drink from the spring? As Winnie is taken away by the Tucks, she sees the man in the yellow suit.

When they stop by a stream for a break, Winnie begins to cry. Mae Tuck reaches into her pocket for her music box, and when it starts to play, it calms Winnie. She decides that "no one who owned a thing like this could be too disagreeable." It is then that the Tucks tell her their story. Eighty-seven years before, the Tuck family had become immortal by drinking water from the magical spring. They didn't know it immediately, but they found out that the water would keep them alive—at the age they were the day they drank it—forever. They will stop at nothing to prevent others from enduring the same fate.

Even though she is not sure whether or not to believe them, Winnie agrees to go home with them until they figure out what to do. Unbeknownst to the whole group, the man in the yellow suit has heard the whole story. When they arrive at the Tucks' house, Winnie meets Mae's husband, Angus Tuck.

Winnie becomes fond of the Tucks as they set out to teach her why it is so important that no one find out about the spring. Each one tries to show her that eternal life is a terrible burden. In the meantime, the man in the yellow suit shows up at the Fosters' door with a deal in mind. He will get Winnie back in exchange for ownership of their wood. Desperate to get Winnie back, her parents agree.

When the man in the yellow suit tells the constable about the deal he's struck with the Fosters, the constable is a little suspicious, but he follows the man to the Tucks, anyway. The man in the yellow suit arrives before the constable, however, and confronts the Tucks with his knowledge. He tells them that his plan is to let the whole world know of this fountain of youth, but that he will only sell the water to people "worthy" of it. He even suggests using the Tucks as examples of the water's effects. The Tucks are outraged at the prospect of being treated like "freaks." The man in the yellow suit takes hold of Winnie and threatens to make her drink the spring water if they refuse to cooperate with him. Mae Tuck grabs Angus's gun and hits the man in the yellow suit over the head with it. The man falls to the ground unconscious.

The constable arrives just in time to see what Mae has done. The Tucks and Winnie try to explain that Mae struck him because he had threatened to take Winnie from them. The constable takes Mae into custody and explains that if the man dies, she will go to the gallows (a structure from which criminals are executed by hanging). At that moment, they realize what will happen if Mae is sent to the gallows. When she doesn't die, the whole world will understand that she can't die and the secret will be out.

The constable returns Winnie to her family. Later she learns that the man in the yellow suit has died. Winnie decides that she must help; she cannot let Mae go to the gallows. The next day Jesse tells her about their plan to help Mae escape at midnight. Jesse also gives Winnie a little bottle of the spring water. He tells her to think about drinking it when she turns seventeen so that they can get married and be together forever.

Before Jesse leaves, Winnie volunteers to help with Mae's escape from jail. At midnight, Winnie sneaks out of her house and meets the Tucks at the prison. Together, they pry off the window frame of the cell so that Mae can get out and Winnie can crawl inside. Winnie then takes Mae's place.

Winnie waits through the night in the cell, hiding under the cot blanket until the constable discovers her in the morning. Although everyone is upset with her, she feels proud of what she has done. She has rescued the Tucks and helped save the world from the dangers and disappointments of eternal life.

In the final chapter, Winnie finds that some people look at her differently now. Because she got into trouble, people are more interested in her.

The book ends with an epilogue in which the Tucks pull into Treegap many years in the future. They learn that the wood has long since been bulldozed and that Winifred Foster has died two years before. They feel sad for Jesse, but they are satisfied that Winnie had decided to live her life as it should be lived, with an end in sight.

Thinking about the plot

- Why is it important for Winnie to understand why she must keep the Tucks' secret?

- How does Winnie's life change through her experiences?

- How do Winnie's decisions affect the outcome of the book?

"The house was so proud of itself that you wanted to make a lot of noise as you passed, and maybe even throw a rock or two. But the wood had a sleeping otherworld appearance that made you want to speak in whispers."

—Tuck Everlasting

Tuck Everlasting takes place in and around a small town named Treegap. Natalie Babbitt does not give us much information about exactly where in the world this town is located. By leaving out specific details about the region, country, or even continent where this story takes place, the author lets the reader know that the location is not the most important part of the book. The events that occur in *Tuck Everlasting* could occur in any ordinary town.

Place

In *Tuck Everlasting*, the description of the surroundings—the town of Treegap, the Fosters' house, the wood, and the Tucks' house—draws the reader into this very special place. In the first chapter the author starts to establish the setting by describing the road that leads to Treegap: "But on reaching the shadows of the first trees, it veered sharply, swung out in a wide arc as if, for the first time, it had reason to think where it was going, and passed around [the wood]." Babbitt traces the road as it wanders along curves, comes to a small hill, and ambles down to a meadow, coming at last to a wood. She wants her reader to know from the start that the town, the wood, and the road are all mentioned on purpose. She wants the reader to sense that somehow the road knew to veer sharply away from the wood and lead elsewhere instead.

On the other side of that wood, she continues, "the sense of easiness dissolved," in the small town on the edge of the wood. "The road no longer belonged to the cows. It became, instead, and rather abruptly, the property of people." At the very edge of Treegap the road goes by the Fosters' cottage. Its "touch-me-not appearance" suggests that its owners do not welcome visitors. The description of the Fosters' house, which is kept in tip-top shape and is run with a great deal of care and attention, gives the reader information about the people who live there.

The Fosters are protective of their property, which Babbitt describes as "surrounded by grass cut painfully to the quick and enclosed by a capable iron fence some four feet high which clearly said, 'Move on—we don't want *you* here.'" In the same chapter, we learn that the Fosters, who own and inhabit that first, proud house, also own the wood. Because it is the property of the Fosters, other people generally leave the wood alone.

In stark contrast to the Fosters' house, the Tucks' house in the wood is described as being in a state of disarray. Babbitt uses their house to represent disorder. Just as the Fosters' house is neat and uninviting, the Tucks' house is terribly messy but warm —just like its inhabitants. The Tucks' house paints a picture of who they are. Warm and welcoming, it is a house filled with the clutter that has accumulated over too much time.

Babbitt makes it clear from the start that "the village itself doesn't matter, except for the jailhouse and the gallows." She lets the reader know that only that first house is important, "the first house, the road, and the wood."

Time

The author gives us some clues about the time period of this novel. Through details like Winnie's high-button shoes and the fact that the characters ride on horseback and in wagons rather than in cars, we know that the story probably takes place in the 1800s. At the very end, we learn the exact year the story takes place when the Tucks come upon Winnie's gravestone. It gives the years of her birth and death: 1870–1948. From this we know that the year she meets the Tucks is 1881 (because she is almost eleven), and that it is 1950 when the Tucks return to Treegap.

The epilogue also reveals how the area has changed with the passage of time. The Tucks are still traveling on horseback. When they pull into Treegap, they are laughed at by a man at a gas station. Babbitt introduces a gas station and a man in "greasy coveralls" to show how things have changed even though the

Tucks have remained exactly the same. The introduction of this new time period reminds us that though the rest of the world, even Treegap, has evolved, the Tucks have not. They *cannot*.

The setting of this story is simple—simple people living in an old-fashioned place and time. Babbitt creates an uncomplicated place for a complicated issue. Perhaps she chose it for that very reason, so that it would be easy to get to the heart of Winnie's dilemma without modern or urban obstacles. If there were computers and airplanes, televisions and shopping malls, it might have been difficult to focus on the essential problems of eternal life. Instead, the setting is uncomplicated—some houses, a dirt road, a jail with gallows, and a wood. The simple setting allows Winnie to talk with a toad, wander off alone into the wood, sit in a rowboat on a pond, and observe the cycle of life up close. Babbitt uses all of this to keep the reader focused on the story line and the dilemma of eternal life.

Thinking about the setting

- Why is the fact that no road goes directly through the wood important?
- What do you think the author means when she writes that the road's "sense of easiness dissolved" at the edge of the wood?
- What descriptive words does the author use to describe the two different environments of the Fosters' home and the Tucks' home?

"Everything's a wheel, turning and turning, never stopping."

—Angus Tuck, *Tuck Everlasting*

T uck *Everlasting* has several themes, or layers of meaning. (The theme of a literary work is its main idea and often is a general statement or opinion about life.) Natalie Babbitt uses metaphors and symbols to make the most important themes clear to the reader. A metaphor is a way of describing one thing by comparing it to something else.

Order versus disorder

Throughout the book there is a constant mention of the order of things. This applies to the order of the Fosters' world, particularly their house. But it also applies to the order of life. All things are born, live, and then die. The Tucks represent an interruption of this order—an eternal interruption of that order to be exact. Babbitt shows this disorder in a few ways. First, when Winnie arrives at their house, she is shocked at the state of disarray it is in: lots of dust and cobwebs, a mouse living in the table drawer, half-completed quilts. The house is a stark contrast to the one Winnie lives in. When she sees all of this, all she can think is:

"Maybe it's because they think they have forever to clean it up." The author uses the disorder to show that Winnie is being exposed to a different way of living for the first time. She lets Winnie follow her thought a little further when Winnie thinks to herself, "Maybe they just don't care!" In fact, later when there are no napkins for her to use to wipe her hands properly, Winnie realizes that in this house it is quite all right to lick the maple syrup off your fingers. "Winnie was never allowed to do such a thing at home, but she had always thought it would be the easiest way. And suddenly the meal seemed luxurious."

The author has accomplished two things. She has set up an orderly world versus a disorderly one, while praising the virtues and the shortcomings of both. In an orderly world, you have to clean up after yourself and keep everything in neat stacks, but the world goes on as it should—everyone living and dying and so on and so on. In the disorderly world, you can lick maple syrup off your hands and throw your clothes on the floor, but the people are stuck forever in one place in their lives. In a way, the disarray of the Tucks' house represents the disarray the world would be in if the secret spring were revealed to the public.

Ultimately, Winnie learns to incorporate some of the Tucks' way of living into her own life, taking certain lessons from her time with them. She realizes that her mother and grandmother are more interesting when they are disheveled from the heat, when they are unable to control the way they are feeling. They are simply hot and they have to let go, "their hair unsettled and their knees loose. It was totally unlike them, this lapse from gentility, and it made them much more interesting." And later, Winnie, too, becomes more interesting. At the beginning, the children in her town think of her merely as an extension of her tailored home. In the end, some of the townspeople find her an intriguing hero. She has come to life for them: "She was a figure of romance to them now, where before she had been too neat, too prissy; almost, somehow, too *clean* to be a real friend."

Natural life cycle

Babbitt uses the image of a wheel in the prologue to point out how the first week of August seems to just hang there, "like the highest seat of a Ferris wheel when it pauses in its turning." The wheel becomes a symbol for life and is used again and again throughout the story. When Winnie and Angus Tuck are in the boat on the pond, he explains to Winnie that his family has fallen off the wheel of life, and that they are in an unnatural state. Angus says: "It's a wheel, Winnie. Everything's a wheel, turning and turning, never stopping. The frogs is part of it, and the bugs, and the fish, and the wood thrush, too. And people. But never the same ones. Always coming in new, always growing and changing, and always moving on. That's the way it *is*."

Winnie begins to comprehend this herself when she sees how the water moves out of the pond and into the ocean. She realizes that the pond water is like life and that while the water moves all around them, she and Angus are stuck in the rowboat. Tuck continues, "That's what us Tucks are, Winnie. Stuck so's we can't move on. We ain't part of the wheel no more. Dropped off, Winnie. Left behind. And everywhere around us, things is moving and growing and changing." And when Winnie, whose mind was suddenly "drowned with understanding of what he was saying," blurts out that she doesn't want to die, Tuck reassures her. "Not now. Your time's not now. But dying's part of the wheel, right there next to being born."

Tuck uses the image of the wheel to make Winnie understand the importance of the cycle of life, just as Babbitt uses the imagery of the wheel again and again to show the reader how the wheel works, how it moves things along as they should be moved.

Independence

Winnie's independence is another important theme in the book. In fact, it is her search for independence that leads her to the wood and ultimately to the Tucks. Then, because of her experience with them and choices she makes, she carves out some independence for herself.

At the start of the book Winnie is frustrated by her family because they watch and care for her so diligently. She wishes she had a sibling to take away some of the attention. She tells the toad that she wants to do something on her own that "would make some kind of difference." She even thinks it would be nice to have a new name.

When Winnie steps toward the wood, noting that she will make a final decision about whether or not to run away permanently once she gets there, she is actually taking her first steps toward independence. She gets braver and more independent with each step she takes. Although she has no choice in the matter when she is kidnapped by the Tucks, she goes with them somewhat willingly, trusting her own instincts about their goodness.

There is a crucial moment, though, when it becomes apparent to the readers that Winnie has done some real growing up. When the constable charges the Tucks with kidnapping, Winnie defends them. She tells the constable that she ran away and that she has gone with them willingly. Although she knows this is a lie, she has made an independent decision about who she will defend.

Later, when Winnie decides to help Mae escape, this sense of newfound independence sweeps over her as she sneaks out of the house at night, defying all of the rules that have been set for her. In fact, it is so easy that "she was struck by the realization that, if she chose, she could slip out night after night without their [her parents'] knowing." Even as guilt comes over her, she reminds herself that she has to help Mae and the whole Tuck family.

Independence comes in the form of choices for Winnie. She chooses to walk through the gate and venture into the wood. She chooses to stay with the Tucks and get to know them. She chooses to defend Mae and eventually to help free her. And in the end, she chooses not to drink from the spring, but to live the way life was meant to be lived, with death as part of the wheel.

Greed

An important theme in this book is greed. In *Tuck Everlasting*, the reader learns that the man in the yellow suit feels that money is the most important thing in the world. The reader also meets the Tuck family, who knows that there is one thing in the world that is much more important than any amount of money: protecting the secret of the magical spring.

The man in the yellow suit is very greedy. He will do anything, including threatening to harm Winnie, to find the source of the Tucks' immortality. He tells the Tucks he will sell the enchanted water "only to certain people, people who deserve it. And it will be very, very expensive." The man in the yellow suit is determined to let the world know about the magical spring. He does not care about the difficulties people would experience if they lived forever. He only thinks about how much money he will make. In the end, it is the man's greed for wealth that leads to his death.

In contrast, Angus and Mae Tuck display a great deal of selflessness. While the man in the yellow suit is selfish and concerned only about increasing his wealth, the Tucks focus on the larger picture: ensuring that no one else suffers the curse of living forever. The Tucks give up a great deal in order to protect their secret. For instance, they don't form relationships with other people so that no one will notice they do not get older. Mae describes how their old friends reacted to the Tucks' staying the same age: "They come to pull back from us. There was talk of witchcraft. Black Magic. Well, you can't hardly blame them, but finally we had to leave the farm." Even though it means living a lonely, difficult life, the Tucks know that they must never reveal their secret.

Thinking about the themes

- What do you think is the most important theme?
- How does the wheel metaphor help you understand the life cycle?
- What is good and what is bad about the prospect of eternal life?
- What is good about death? Does it make us see life differently?
- How long would you like to live?

Characters: Who Are These People, Anyway?

"I cast my characters out of the possibilities—the kinds of people who are best going to be able to talk about my idea. The Tuck family has four members, and they were chosen specifically to talk about different points of view of living forever."

—Natalie Babbitt

In some books, the characters' names are simply names the author likes for one reason or another, or names that are appropriate for the setting and the time. Not so for Natalie Babbitt's characters. Babbitt said, "That's one of the things I like the best! In most of my books, the characters' names have secondary meanings that the reader doesn't have to know. In *Tuck Everlasting,* Winnie's last name—Foster—means 'forester.' The name *Tuck* came from a thesaurus and an old dictionary. I wanted a name that meant life and was only one syllable. When I looked it up in my old dictionary, I found that *tuck* meant life. The first names in that book were chosen to go with the times— they're old-fashioned. You don't meet too many people with those names very often anymore—although once I was approached by a woman who told me her name was Winifred Foster!"

Here is a list of the characters in *Tuck Everlasting*, followed by a brief description.

Winifred Foster	a ten-year-old girl, called Winnie
Mae Tuck	the mother of Jesse and Miles, wife of Angus
Angus Tuck	the father of Jesse and Miles, Mae's husband
Miles Tuck	the older son of the Tucks
Jesse Tuck	the younger son of the Tucks
The man in the yellow suit	a man who wants to own the magical spring
The constable	the lawman who arrests Mae Tuck
The Fosters	Winnie's family, which includes her father, mother, and grandmother

Winnie Foster: Winnie Foster, the main character in *Tuck Everlasting*, is a ten-year-old girl who lives a sheltered life in a small town. Her family is wealthy and reserved. She has no siblings and no friends to speak of. When we meet her in the beginning of the novel, she is lonely and bored. She wants to do something with her life, to have an adventure. She begins to consider this in a conversation with a toad that lurks across the road from her front yard. She tells him that she is tired of being watched by her family every second of the day and wants to be herself for once. She tells him she wants to "make some kind of difference in the world."

Winnie is somewhat torn, though. When she sets out into the wood that next day, she is unsure of what to do. She won't commit to running away but thinks she'll see how she feels as she goes. It turns out she doesn't have to make a decision herself. Her life changes the moment she encounters Jesse Tuck in the wood.

Because Winnie is curious and open to new things, she doesn't walk away when she spies Jesse sitting by the spring. Instead, she watches him intensely, and soon finds herself on an adventure that changes her life. At first she is excited about her new experiences. "They were friends, *her* friends. Closing the gate on her oldest fears as she had closed the gate of her own fenced yard, she discovered the wings she's always wished she had. And all at once she was elated." Later, though, she becomes overwhelmed and scared. "She had never slept in any bed but her own in her life. All these thoughts flowed at once from the dark part of her mind. She put down her fork and said, unsteadily, 'I want to go home.'" Winnie continues to go back and forth regarding her feelings for the Tucks and the situation she has gotten into with them. Her emotions become more complicated. She is at once scared and sympathetic, overjoyed and distressed.

But mostly, Winnie is perceptive, very understanding, intelligent, and brave. We first become aware of her perceptiveness when the man in the yellow suit comes to her house and she is reminded of funeral ribbons. She somehow knows that he brings trouble. That same intuition makes her empathetic as well. She feels deeply for the Tucks, and is pained when she notices sadness in them.

But it is Winnie's courage that changes her life. She has lived through something and learned from the experience, and she feels surer of herself for it. At the beginning, she doesn't even know whether or not to run away. In the end, she starts making independent decisions. When she sneaks out of the house and risks everything to save Mae, she not only displays her newfound independence, but also shows she has learned how to be a friend.

Mae Tuck: Mae Tuck is a wife and mother who cares deeply about her family. She tries very hard to keep her family intact. Mae is also very brave. It is she who saves her family and Winnie when she hits the man in the yellow suit over the head. She is a protector. Mae will stop at nothing to prevent others from taking on the burden of eternal life. She is kind, loving, optimistic, and resilient—she has led a long and sometimes difficult life, but still has energy to spare. All of those qualities are evident when she says to Winnie, "Life's got to be lived, no matter how long or short. You got to take what comes."

Angus Tuck: Angus Tuck, called Tuck, is a kind but sad man, who "almost never smiled except in his sleep." For that is when he dreams of heaven and is relieved to be able to forget for a minute that he will live forever. But the "melancholy creases of his cheeks" are displaced by a smile when he meets Winnie Foster. Perhaps most affected of all the Tucks by the curse of eternal life, Tuck hides himself away from the world so that he doesn't have to watch it grow past him. Because he cannot die, he doesn't feel alive. He responds with sheer amazement to Winnie when he meets her. Winnie is alive to him because she will mature and grow old, and eventually die. It makes him feel alive to be near her.

He tells Winnie, "You can't have living without dying. So you can't call it living, what we got. We just *are*, we just *be*, like rocks beside the road." Winnie responds to Tuck's descriptions of immortality most of all. Her empathy comes out when she notices his creased forehead at the breakfast table and when he stares with envy at the man in the yellow suit when he is on the verge of death. Winnie knows that Tuck is in pain.

Natalie Babbitt has said that Angus Tuck is the most important character in the book. "He is the one whose advice Winnie follows."

Miles Tuck: Miles Tuck is "solid, like an oar," according to Winnie. He is broad and muscled and has dirt under his nails from working as a blacksmith to earn money. He had a wife and children who left him when they realized he would not age and he is sad that they could never know why. Instead, they lived and died as he could not and he sees that as tragic. Serious and diligent, Miles wants to do something important with his time someday. He tries to explain the importance of the cycle of life to Winnie when she goes out in the rowboat with him. There, she learns that he is critical of his father's decision to hide from the world, and of Jesse's indulgent lifestyle. He thinks everyone ought to make himself or herself useful.

Jesse Tuck: Jesse Tuck is a seventeen-year-old boy who'll be seventeen forever and doesn't seem to mind one bit. He thinks that if you're destined to live forever, you might as well enjoy it. Winnie thinks he is the opposite of Miles and likens him to "water: thin and quick." He is optimistic, hopeful, and free-spirited. Winnie develops a crush on him. At first, she admires him because he is handsome and charming. Later, she adores him because he seems to like her, too. He wants Winnie to drink from the spring when she is seventeen and then marry him so they can live forever, together.

The man in the yellow suit: The man in the yellow suit represents the dark side of the Tucks' situation. He wants to exploit them by treating them like a sideshow. He has no morals. He doesn't see the Tucks as people, but as objects put on earth to make him rich. He refuses to see the consequences of his plan. Natalie Babbitt has explained:

> Every fantasy has to have a villain. The MITYS is based on somebody that I actually knew . . . a completely amoral, hugely powerful, completely selfish person. We are used to villains that know what good is and go against it. The MITYS does not concern himself with good or bad. The only thing he thinks about is what he wants, without regard to what it might mean philosophically or to people's lives.

Thinking about the characters

- Which of the Tucks do you feel closest to? Why?
- Would you like to have Winnie for a friend? Why or why not?
- Do you feel differently about Mae Tuck after she kills the man in the yellow suit? Why or why not?

"Flawless"

When *Tuck Everlasting* was first published in 1975, the reviews were exceptional. A reviewer for *The Horn Book* wrote, "Rarely does one find a book with such distinctive prose. Flawless in both style and structure, it is rich in imagery and punctuated with light fillips of humor." The reviewer was not only impressed with the beautiful language that Natalie Babbitt used, but also by the funny moments she included.

A review in *Harper's* stated that *Tuck Everlasting* was "probably the best work of our best children's novelist." Evidently many people agree with this statement because it was named one of the most important children's books of the twentieth century by *School Library Journal*. It is so popular, in fact, that it was made into a feature film that was released in 2002.

Some people who have read the book feel that despite its historical setting, children many years in the future will also enjoy *Tuck Everlasting*. A review from *Booklist* stated that "with its serious intentions, and light touch the story is, like the Tucks, timeless."

Controversy about the ending

Though most readers agree that the book is marvelous, others have had a negative response to the ending. They feel that Winnie should have taken a drink from the spring and found Jesse and lived with him forever. But, as Natalie Babbitt has explained, usually even the most critical reader comes around eventually. (See Natalie Babbitt's story on page 11 about a reader who changed her mind.)

In addition, some people feel that Babbitt's description of the Tuck family is not entirely realistic. A reviewer from the *New York Times Book Review* wrote that the Tucks were "nice people; their unshakable niceness is perhaps the only really unlikely part of the story." The Tucks have lived a very, very long time and experienced great loss due to their immortality. This reviewer finds it difficult to believe the Tucks could be so kind to Winnie after suffering for so long.

Thinking about what others think of *Tuck Everlasting*
• How do you feel about the ending?
• Do you think *Tuck Everlasting* deserves all the praise?
• Do you think the book's historical setting will help the story remain appealing for years to come? Why or why not?

Glossary

Here are some important words used in *Tuck Everlasting.* Some are common words that have uncommon meanings. Understanding them will make it easier to read the novel.

acrid bitter or unpleasant to the smell or taste

bovine having qualities characteristic of a cow

cahoots in partnership

catholic involving or concerning all of humankind

colander a cooking utensil with holes used for rinsing or draining food

constable a lawman

cross angry

ebbed fell back or receded

eddies currents of water moving in a circular motion

elation a feeling of extreme joy or pride

embankment a raised structure that prevents water from overflowing

exasperated irritated or out of patience

furrowed wrinkled with deep grooves

galling causing extreme irritation

gallows a frame from which condemned people were hanged

gypsies wandering people

illiterate unable to read or write

indomitable impossible to tame or subdue

jaunty showy

kingfisher a brightly colored bird

marionette a wooden figure made to move from above by strings attached to its jointed limbs

melancholy deep sadness or depression

metaphysics the philosophical study of being and knowing

parson a member of the clergy

petulance the quality of being ill-tempered

plaintive mournful

ponderous heavy or important

prostrate to reduce to extreme weakness; to be overcome

roust to wake up someone or disturb

rueful expressing sorrow or regret

searing burning or scorching

self-deprecation the act of putting oneself down

staunchly in a firm way

tangent a sudden change of course

teeming overflowing

threadbare shabby

verandah a porch or balcony

"I write for children because I am interested in fantasy and the possibilities for experience of all kinds before the time of compromise. I believe that children are far more perceptive and wise than American books give them credit for being."

—Natalie Babbitt

Although Natalie Babbitt started out as an illustrator, she has said, "Now writing is far more important to me than illustrating, for it seems clear that the things I have to say I can say much more effectively with words than I ever could with pictures, in spite of old maxims to the contrary." (As the saying goes, "A picture is worth a thousand words.") Babbitt says that it was all the reading she did as a child that led her to a career in illustrations and, ultimately, writing for children. She believes that it is because she loves words that she is able to use them so effectively in her writing.

Natalie once wrote an essay called, "My Love Affair with the Alphabet." It is about how miraculous the alphabet is. She wonders "how those twenty-six funny shapes can group themselves in endlessly different ways to make words with endlessly different meanings." The essay expresses her opinion that the letters of the alphabet on the pages of a book enable us to go to different places, to be someone else entirely, and to accomplish extraordinary things.

For aspiring writers

Natalie Babbitt has said that if you really want to be a writer, you should probably be a reader first. She believes that it is by reading stories that you learn to tell them well. "All of us are storytellers of one kind or another, and I wish you all lots of luck with it if you choose to do it."

It was through her observation of other people's writing experiences that she learned an important lesson she likes to share with aspiring writers:

> My husband took time out from his academic career to write a novel and discovered that he didn't enjoy the long, lonely hours that writing demanded. My sister produced a comic novel, which required substantial rewriting. I learned three valuable things from observing my husband's and sister's forays into the writer's world: You have to give writing your full attention. You have to like the revision process. And you have to like to be alone. But it was years before I put any of this to good use.

- **Write the sequel:** Don't you wish you knew what became of Jesse Tuck? Write a story about what happened to Jesse after Mae was freed. How long did he wait for Winnie? Did he fall in love again? Did he get into any trouble? Where do you think he traveled?

- **Be a reporter:** The town of Treegap was certainly in a tizzy the day after Mae's escape from the jail. What might the local newspaper have said of the mysterious circumstances surrounding her disappearance? You be the reporter who gets the story. Interview the townsfolk. Did anyone see anything? Has anyone heard any rumors? Perhaps someone has some gossip to include about Winnie's affection for Jesse Tuck...

- **The legend of Treegap Spring:** Doesn't the eternal life-giving spring remind you of an old legend? How do you think it became enchanted in the first place? Was it elves after all? Use your imagination to come up with a magical story about the history of the spring.

- **Keep a diary:** Imagine that you suddenly find out that you are going to stay the age you are today forever. Start a fictional diary. Start your diary on the day you become immortal. How did it happen? At an encounter with a magical being? Or perhaps after finding an unusual object? Were you with any of your friends or family members? What is it like to see your friends get older? Since you'll never appear older, will you be in the same grade forever? Write a few sentences each day about who you reveal your secret to, what is good about living forever, and what you don't enjoy about it, and anything else that you think is interesting about your new situation.

• **Write as Natalie Babbitt:** Part of what makes this book so special is the wonderful imagery the author uses to describe the simplest objects and situations. Write a story of your own and try using similes, metaphors, and personification the way Natalie Babbitt does. These literary tools will help your writing come alive!

• **Write an advertisement:** If the man in the yellow suit had lived, he would have had to advertise the spring water in order to sell it. Make a poster advertising the water. What would it say? How would he persuade people to pay for the water?

Activities

- **You be the judge!:** Imagine Mae Tuck hadn't been able to escape. What might her trial have been like? Would the jury believe her story or would they sympathize with the man in the yellow suit? Have a mock trial and find out! You will need a judge, a jury of twelve people, a prosecutor, a defense lawyer, and witnesses for Mae Tuck.

- **Words that paint a picture:** Natalie Babbitt is an artist as well as a writer. Are you? Let's find out! Read over some of your favorite descriptions in the book, and try to draw or paint the scene. Maybe it's the winding road, or the entrance to the wood, or the spring, or the Tucks' house on the pond . . .

- **Back to the future:** When the Tucks return to Treegap in the epilogue, they find the town very different. What would your town look like if you were to return in one hundred years? What has changed? What has stayed the same?

- **Watch the movie:** *Tuck Everlasting,* the movie, came out in 2002 and is now available on video and DVD. Get a group of friends together and watch it. Then, have a "movie group." Talk about how the movie is different from the book. Did everyone like it? Which did you like better?

- **Get a library card:** If you already have a card, head to the library and check out some of Natalie Babbitt's other stories! If you don't have a library card, make sure to get one. You will find endless possibilities for great reading inside the library!

- **Make some flapjacks!:** With the help of an adult, you can enjoy flapjacks just like the Tucks and Winnie did!

Ingredients

3 tablespoons butter
1½ cups all-purpose flour
2 tablespoons brown sugar
1½ teaspoons baking powder
½ teaspoon salt
1½ cups milk
2 large eggs
1 tablespoon of maple or regular syrup
½ teaspoon vanilla

Directions

1. Melt the butter, either in a small pan on the stove or in a small bowl in the microwave. Let the melted butter cool for several minutes.

2. In a large mixing bowl, combine flour, brown sugar, baking powder, and salt. Mix together with a whisk (a fork will work, too) so it is well combined.

3. In a separate small bowl, combine the melted butter, milk, eggs, syrup, and vanilla. Whisk these ingredients together.

4. Add the liquid mixture to the flour mixture. Whisk together until there are no big chunks of flour. The batter will be lumpy, not smooth. Do not mix too much or else the flapjacks won't be fluffy.

5. Grease the griddle or pan with oil or butter. You could use cooking spray if you prefer.

6. With an adult's help, heat up a griddle or large pan on high heat on the stove.

7. With a ladle or measuring cup, pour about ⅓ cup of batter onto the skillet.

8. When the top is covered in bubbles and a few begin to pop, turn over the pancake using a rubber or metal spatula.

9. Cook for about one minute more and lift up an edge to check to see if it's done. The flapjack should be golden brown.

10. Top with butter and syrup!

Other books by Natalie Babbitt

Bub; Or the Very Best Thing (1994)

The Devil's Other Storybook (1987)

The Devil's Storybook (1974)

Dick Foote and the Shark (1967)

Elsie Times Eight (2001)

The Eyes of the Amaryllis (1977)

Goody Hall (1971)

Herbert Rowbarge (1982)

Kneeknock Rise (1970)

Nellie, a Cat on Her Own (1989)

Ouch! (1998)

Phoebe's Revolt (1968)

The Search for Delicious (1969)

The Something (1970)

Books illustrated by Natalie Babbitt

All the Small Poems by Valerie Worth (1987)

All the Small Poems and Fourteen More by Valerie Worth (1994)

The Big Book for Peace by Alexander Lloyd (1990)

Curlicues, the Fortunes of Two Pug Dogs by Valerie Worth (1980)

The Forty-Ninth Magician by Samuel Babbitt (1966)

More Small Poems by Valerie Worth (1976)

Other Small Poems Again by Valerie Worth (1986)

Peacock and Other Poems by Valerie Worth (2002)

Small Poems by Valerie Worth (1972)

Small Poems Again by Valerie Worth (1986)

Still More Small Poems by Valerie Worth (1978)

Movies

Tuck Everlasting (2002)

Bibliography

Books

Babbitt, Natalie. *Tuck Everlasting.* New York: Farrar, Straus and Giroux, 1975.

dePaola, Tomie, and others. *Once Upon a Time ... Celebrating the Magic of Children's Books in Honor of the Twentieth Anniversary of Reading Is Fundamental.* New York: G. P. Putnam's Sons, 1986.

Silvey, Anita. *The Essential Guide to Children's Books and Their Creators.* Boston: Houghton Mifflin, 2002.

Newspapers and magazines

Booklist, volume 72, December 1, 1975, p. 510.

The Bulletin of the Center for Children's Books. "True Blue: Natalie Babbitt." June 1999.

Horn Book, volume 52, February 1976, p. 47.

New York Times Book Review, November 16, 1975, pp. 32, 56.

School Library Journal, volume 22, December 1975, p. 50.

Web sites

The Bulletin of the Center for Children's Books:
http://alexia.lis.uiuc.edu/puboff/bccb/0699true.html

Cedar Falls Public Library Youth Department:
www.cedar-falls.lib.ia.us/youth/author3.html

Disney:
http://disney.go.com/disneypictures/tuck

Educational Paperback Association:
www.edupaperback.org

Kidspace @ The Internet Public Library:
http://www.ipl.org/div/kidspace/askauthor/babbitt.html

Kidsreads.com:
http://www.kidsreads.com/authors/au-babbitt-natalie.asp

Scholastic:
http://www2.scholastic.com/teachers/authorsandbooks/
authorstudies/authorstudies.jhtml